After the Rain

Julie Missen

Published 2025 by Carrot Press
Book cover and image design by Carrot
Publishing

Also By The Author

Fiction

Confessions From A Fractured Mind

Detective Inspector Morgan Series:

Secrets From A Misty River

The Evil Within Us All

The Legend Of The Bawdsey Boys

Poetry

Love, Death and Madness

Childrens

The Little Mole

The Little Spider

For my children,

my constant reminder of life after the rain

Contents

A Woodland Walk

We meander alongside
the bubbling brook
that takes us through
dappled autumn shades,
when two grey squirrels
racing between gnarled, bent trunks
lead our steps astray
to a cool glade,
hidden well from the path
that we have drifted from
and into the arms of the murderous crows
whose sinister caws' warned long
before we dared to step inside
a place where we do not belong.

Napping On A Summers Afternoon

Green shoots,

budding life,

brings forth all hope of warm summer nights

and lazy naps in the midday sun,

chorused by sparrows

flitting, through leaf-laden branches

that stretch upwards towards the sky;

an offering to the sun,

worshipped long

before I was born.

Water trickles through tiny palms

plunged deep into pits of yellow grain,

molded into a minds vision

of castles, long since gone.

A buzzing bee distracts

from the task at hand,

crushed creations left

hurriedly, discarded in the sand.

The drone of a nearby mower

invokes sleep, at last

and shaded from the searing heat

by the fronds of a Chinese Palm,

the sounds of summer fade to a lull

as all consciousness are now calmed.

Crocuses In The Snow

Lilac delights appear through pure white snow,

lying thickly on fronds of grass so pure,

green shoots push through

last autumns leaves,

searching, upwards,

soldiers upstanding, forthright,

winding clear of obstruction

through clods of grain

that cannot hold back

the tides of spring

spreading across the land.

Camelia In The Rain

Deep russet hues
caressed by droplets
so gently, they do not fall
but cling, tight
to the fragile beauty
that cups them
for safe keeping
until the dawn
fades them from view,
returned to whence they came
until the soft pillows overflow once more
and melt into the gentle patter of rain.

A Walk Through Life

Crystals glisten
on the pure-lily snow
that lightly covers
the path whence I go.
Onward, crisp footsteps
crunch across the frost
covered fields
that lead me
to where, I don't know.
Biting winds
blow all thoughts of presence past
and shield the future
from the mind
that concentrates only
on the path that is now mine.
Trudging, forward,
a shimmering moon
lights my way
through the tangled undergrowth
that snarls at my feet

and tries to hold me steadfast

from the fate I might meet;

alone in the dark.

A directionless haze

settles across this lonely stroll,

through the thick maze

eventually, I find my way home.

Almost

I almost wish I were
an autumn leaf,
floating down stream
near the fishing spot,
where once I did dream.
Or a Wren, flitting
amongst the trees
in the ancient woods,
where dens were built from logs.
Or a dragonfly, buzzing over the pond
where black nets caught newts
but never the frogs.
Nostalgic memories of days no longer here
almost makes me wish
to be back as we once were.

After The Rain

Fresh beginnings;
cleanse the past of its sins,
caress memories, long past,
nurture growth with a hope
that was once cast aside.
The road we took
left a bitterness inside,
never foretold, yet never forgot;
a peace of mind
denied.

A scent anew;
spring lambs amongst the daffodils,
frolic askew until maturity tempers
the joyfulness, once remembered
is hidden, still, in shallow graves
where snowdrops grow
near the churchyard nave,
all now washed away
by the morning rain.

Conception

One brief moment
is all that it takes
of lust, of love
or even of hate.
Thoughtless misgivings
the weakened resolve,
yearning to be touched;
to surrender our love
to another's trust.

That one brief moment
where I loved
and felt loved
and hated my insecurities.
A shared passion
that only some will know,
a split second of time
was all that made you.

Gestation

Growing, budding,
pushing, squeezing
into space that is not theirs.
These aliens breed,
living, parasitically,
destroying their hosts,
sucking on their food,
breathing in their air,
these egotistical creatures
are difficult to bear.
Fighting for space,
clawing for room,
pushing aside the swollen womb,
no thoughts for mother,
only for themselves,
these selfish creatures
scream 'love me, love me',
for I need you
to make me 'me'.

Birth

Creating life;
life creates itself.
Pushing forth from the happy womb
into the cold dark world
to the bosom of its' mother.
Sucking on life's essence,
breathing in the world.

Baby

Microscopic digits curl around my own,
unseeing eyes search around the room,
sounds, oh so new
trigger distant memories from the womb.
Helpless, alone, no thoughts for you,
no concept of love or understanding of truth.
A meal machine, a processing factory
to be trained and denied for our society.
A wealth of freedom to remain unknown,
another soldier to serve in our home.

Children

The innocents;
the young ones,
perfect carbon copies
of who we once were.
Pure and untainted;
a new day, begun.

Mother's left

Mother's left.
Provider and destroyer
she gives all
takes all away
and leaves us
with nothing.
An emptiness
cannot be replaced,
a bitterness
I cannot hide.

No Mother, No More

No Mother no more;
no more cups of tea in bed
no more stories to be read
no more comfort when I am sick
nor Saturday shopping trips
no praise for achievements
no hugs for disappointments
no surprise presents
just for being good,
no mother
no more.

A Childhood Left Behind

A forgotten toy
left, unloved in the corner of the room.
The once-prized possession
fades from view
replaced, in time
with something shiny;
something new.

A furry creature, too old to play
left alone to slowly decay
until its death releases the guilt
of a once-loved pet
that has been all but forgot,
behind a closed door
it is left to rot.

The one-eye bear, once so prized,
squeezed so hard it popped out one of its eyes,
now lost under the bed with monsters of old
that lurk unremembered,

their stories now untold
of shadows, dark,
that kept small eyes from sleeping,
now banished to a dusty shelf
when once they lived
in the imaginations of tiny children,
who feared to sleep,
lest they never awaken.

And now the most import of fixtures
that once held centre court,
is relegated to taxi driver
and an ever-deepening purse
by the once small child,
gently nursed through fevered nights
and days, filled with wonder
in equal measure.
Now torn asunder from the warm safe place
that sprung forth the feathered fledging,
whose tentative flight was keenly nurtured
until confidence prevailed it out into the world
with a bond that slackens then cuts loose,

untethered from the once-needed nest,

now lays empty, forgotten.

And the once cherished bear,

previously never discarded,

lays unused, unwanted in a cobwebbed

cupboard

of forgotten childhood things.

Nestled against an empty cage

the one-eye bear sits alone,

an unseen tear trickling down its cheek

as it waits for the day

when another child,

chooses to make it

their very best thing.

First Love, Forever

You were there in the spring of my life;
soft kisses on the grassy strip
between the amusement arcade and the prom,
those deep brown eyes drew me to a safe place
that I was longing to find.
A tantalising glimpse of sweet love
before you snatched it away
with your cruel denial
that we were anything more than friends.
You were there again in the summer
when I had flourished into my own truth
with a more confident façade, but still,
the flicker of that first love refused to fade
and made swift my decision
to let you back into my life.
You were broken, a ghost of the lad I once knew,
reaching out for hope from the darkness
that had consumed you,
but I could not help, I didn't know how to.
You came back once more in the autumn

when my life had started over,

and the hope still held of our young love

brought me to trust you again, but still,

you could not bring yourself to let me

kiss the tears on the cheeks

I once knew so well,

instead, you turned away

and disappeared once again.

And now as the winter of my life

is drawing ever nearer,

I cannot help but wonder if you will reappear

and let me gaze once more

into those beautiful deep brown eyes

that have forever held my love

since the first time that we kissed;

in front of the amusement arcade

with the echo of the waves

crashing onto the beach behind us.

The place where I will always remember,

a love that was never really mine.

Petals in the Wind

A pleasure softly held
gone too soon,
falling through empty fingers
that once held onto you.
Pools of faded
once-glinting lights
now sallow deep,
in cheeks, pale, jaded,
once flushed with pleasure
from a love
that I could not keep.
We are all petals in the wind;
a fleeting delight
in the river
of life.

Silence Cuts

The silence cuts

through my deepest fears

that nestle, cupped

in whitened hands.

Sharp edges

that tear at the flesh,

releasing beads of burgundy

that are measured

only by my tears

that fall for you.

Dreaming Of A Long-Ago Lover

I dreamt of you,
sitting on my sofa
as if the years had not passed
between us.
I remember still,
that youthful longing
of a cottage by the sea,
where you would paint
and I would write.
Whatever happened to this childish dream
of a simple life, a quiet existence
that we always believed
would one day be ours.
Perhaps it may still.
I pick up my pen and stare at the blank page in
front of me,
as I wait in the cottage by the sea
for you to come home.

No Lover, No More

No lover, no more;
no sweet affair
no roses for love
no security for fear
no comfort in bed
when winter nights are long
no candlelit dinners
or cherished love song,
no lover
no more.

Crushed Fruit

Hatred, prickles
at the sight of you;
a reminder of the misery that we endured
at your vile hand
that crushed and squeezed
fruit, peachy soft,
molded, de-flowered
by fingers, so cruel
whose only joy
was to erase the very essence
that made us who
we once were,
before
we
met
you.

Separation, Never

I never escaped.
8 years in and I never escaped
I just thought that I did.
In my head I was free,
I was where I dreamt I'd be;
a life anew, a future redrawn blank,
full of possibilities.
An illusion of happiness
soon replaced with
a hope laid flat
by the realisation,
I can no longer deny,
that I never escaped,
I am trapped
until I die.

My Life in Boxes

Stacked high
with no care for their content,
memories pressed
into tiny spaces
waiting to be exhumed.
A tense longing
for change to come,
coupled by an odd loyalty for days gone by,
forever stored in these boxes.
Old and new,
thrown together, a delicious mix
of a life story with blank pages to come.
Who knows where this life will turn to next.

Leaving the Mausoleum

The once marital home
now entombed in the past,
ghostly hands that hold tight,
preventing all thoughts of escape
clutch tightly onto lost dreams
that flutter and fade;
dust fairies in the wind,
caught in a sun beam
that squeezes through
the dense fog of my mind.
Warmth on upturned cheeks
brings attention again
to the task at hand that seems endless,
unforgiving;
a chastisement of failure,
a reminder of hopes now discarded
into the grey-lidded bin
overflowing with objects from a former life,
no longer cherished but a thorn
that prickles the vein with disappointment

seemingly, never shall pass

through time, flowers fade;

a transparent grey that reminds of the death

that has transpired

of a marriage, of a home

of a once planned out future.

A shadow of my former self

to be left behind

as I step out into the bright sunlight

across the threshold that once brought joy

and onto a new path, a new journey;

a new place, I will call home.

School Days Revisited

As I step into the room
the years fade in seconds.
Nothing has changed.
The creases around your eyes have deepened
but still, that dull gaze stares back at me,
questioning, without asking,
why are you here?
Swallowing hard, I fight to contain
the forgotten feelings of inadequacy
that have never left, only faded from view
for a little while,
they have stayed, lurking
waiting to surface again
at first sight of you.
I am a girl again
standing on the edge,
reluctant to leave,
unable to break through
the inner circle
where I never belonged.

Always, teetering on the edge,
never invited in,
nor sent away,
an excruciating limbo that always stays;
Rapunzels tower, never to be climbed
dwarfs my fragile ego,
reminding me that I am nothing
to you
and never will be.

Maternal Love

I would give you the moon
if it were within my grasp.
Every breath that leaves my body
runs through you
in your every moment
from the first beat of your heart
until the very last.
Wherever I may be
I will be with you, always,
wiping away your tears,
sitting at the end of your bed
through sleepless nights
and every day
that I am needed
I am there
with you.

A Shining Light

Do not hide your shining light
from those who would keep you small,
nor bow down to the same level
of those who wish you not to grow tall.
Stand resolute against the darkness;
a north star of morning light
that spreads its brilliance
across the moonlit night.
Hold your voice, clear and strong
against those who would silence your dreams,
for when you do, you will surely find
the place where you belong.

My Daughters Eyes

Dark pools that reveal
generations of memories
unspoken, all knowing
of what went before.
Glistening, bright dew drops
that know no beginning
nor end, for time is infinite;
wise words, unspoken
need not be heard
but are passed on, cherished
through every deed done
and of every that is still to come.

The Book

A pure love;
a true love that knows no bounds
or conditions on its' entity,
is as rare as an ancient text
found hidden, in a treasure chest.
Fragile bindings that threaten to crumble
if held too tightly or too roughly travelled.
Smooth pages that wrinkle as time passes,
creased by life's twists and turns
that hurry the demise of a once-white page.
Yellowed with age by life's experience,
its' knowledge embodied within these pages
divulge a journey,
an offering of wisdom to pass on
to the generations of love that will surely come;
to nurture, softly, these brittle bones
held together now by surfaced veins
that reveal a gentleness, a strength contained
within these bonds that we call love.

Reminders of Love

What is love,
but a fleeting moment of happiness;
a murmur on the breeze
that carries you away from me.
It is a memory, long held,
it is tears from the past,
and an upturned smile
that leaps my heart from its' frozen chasm
into hope, but for the shallowest flutter
before it crashes down, snaffled
deep inside, this hollow chamber
that once beat
with every drum that joy can bring.
And it is the whisper of the wind
through the barest of trees
entirely shed of yesteryears leaves,
it is the gentle fall of snow-covered fields
whose footprints lead a path
through darkened skies
and returns to light, this heavy heart

stilled, by the distance that time brings.

Then, all is vanquished by a moments glance

at the memories that replenish this lonely heart,

through these reminders

of what love is.

When the Clock Strikes Midnight on New Years Eve

For old acquaintances, never forgot,
still there sitting in the smoke-filled pub,
Jukebox paused at ten seconds to go,
poppers held at the ready, silly hat askew,
eyes shining with a glassy dew,
kissed cheeks, sticky shoes,
even a hand shake or two,
then a glass is raised for those that we've lost,
still sitting there in the smoke-filled pub,
they never left,
these ghosts of mine, of yours,
forever snapped in that moment before their life
was paused.
Our old acquaintances
never forgot.

Thoughts of Death

Sinking

down

into a velveteen chasm

of sweet nothingness.

Caressing,

smoothing sharp corners,

rounding hard edges that tear and bruise,

molding,

shaping,

stretching into a formless shape;

pliable,

new.

Calming,

slowing,

floating into the blissful beyond,

melting into peace;

a myriad of souls,

a meeting of minds,

a sense of belonging,

an enticement, of love.

Time Ticking

Time is not my friend;

pulling me ever closer to death,

tick, tick, tick

the silent hands move

smoothly, with no bumps in the road

down the infinite path,

darkness, encasing,

a void, shallow.

The rustle of the wind

calls to us,

chills our minds;

a reminder of life's finality,

a future,

that

is

not

mine.

A Deathbed Goodbye

A life fades so easily
but still, the layers of memories
peel back the distance
bringing us closer once again,
If only for a brief moment.
A shared treasure,
we cling onto tight
as the light slips into the night
and draws your breath from living.
A slowing of mind, a calm descends,
an acceptance that all has changed
and will never be the same again.
In the next moment
I am left with only memories.

I Am, Always, Forever

I am the rock
that holds fast against the tide,
white foam that coverts greyness,
conical limpets clamped down, steadfast
against currents that will not abide.
I am the slender stalk of wheat
that sways in the bitter wind
but does not break, instead returning
for the daybreak that comes again.
I am the gentle brook
that trickles over time
from a past that's all forgot;
of a life that was once mine.
I am the leaf that carries away
the words I wish to say,
that hides in russet hues,
skeletal thinness that decays.
And I am the memory
that lives on forever more
in every blade of grass

that pushes through winter straw,

and in the gentle snowdrops, pure

that signal springs beginnings;

sheltered by sentries of yellow gold

that protect, always

the words I long to say

that now are etched in stone,

where they will stay forever,

unheard.

About The Author

This is Julie's second poetry book, the first, 'Love, Death and Madness' was published in 2024 by Carrot Press. Julie is also the author of the Detective Inspector Morgan series, which is set in her home county of Suffolk. Julie has also written and published psychological thrillers and children's books.

www.ingramcontent.com/pod-product-compliance
Lightning Source LLC
Chambersburg PA
CBHW060056050426
42448CB00011B/2492